# EFFECTIVE TELEPHONE COMMUNICATION SKILLS

## Mia Schiffman Melanson

## Help Desk Institute

Help Desk Institute
6385 Corporate Drive, Suite 301
Colorado Springs, CO 80919 USA
U.S. and Canada: (800) 248-5667
www.ThinkHDI.com

# Table of Contents

# About the Author

Mia Schiffman Melanson has extensive experience within sales and support organizations, both as manager and consultant. For the past seventeen years, she has developed and delivered training in customer service, telemarketing, coaching and supervisory skills for entrepreneurial organizations and Fortune 500 companies.

Through her consulting firm, Marketing Mastery & Training, Mia works primarily with professionals in high customer contact functions where performance impacts profit on a daily basis. Ms. Melanson also teaches and evaluates students at Northeastern University's Graduate School of Business where she is an adjunct faculty member.

Before founding her own company, she was Marketing Manager at Prime Computer, where she was responsible for both strategic and tactical aspects of marketing campaigns, generating measurable revenue for the company and earning her an Excellence award. She is a member of Who's Who in the World (1996) and New England Women Business Owners.

# Chapter 1

*Why good telephone communication
skills benefit your organization*

For years. Support Center managers have been tasked with
maintaining and improving the high-tech skills of the Support
Center staff. By *high-tech skills*, I mean product knowledge and
problem-solving skills. These skills are vital since the primary
task of support agents is to solve customers' technical problems.

In recent years, however, the importance of *high-touch skills* has
become more fully recognized. *High-touch skills*, or communication
skills, are primarily speaking and listening skills. This book
focuses on high-touch skills and offers your organization some
simple and efficient ways to improve them.

This chapter explores the reasons why effective telephone
communication skills are needed at your organization. Chapter
2 explains "How we create our image over the telephone."
In that chapter, you'll review the components of telephone
communication and the importance of your tone of voice.
Chapter 3 gives you practical, easy-to-use advice, including
do's and don'ts, on how to become a better listener over the
telephone. Then Chapter 4 delves into what it takes to be a
good speaker over the telephone. The practical advice and
valuable do's and don'ts are simple ways of improving your
communication skills.

## The customer relationship composite

Figure 1-1 shows a model that I call the "customer relationship composite." In this composite, you'll see the various skills that influence interactions with customers. Speaking skills and listening skills represent the two high-touch needs, while problem-solving skills and product knowledge represent the two high-tech needs. All the components function in a two-way manner. In other words, both the agent and the customer exhibit all four skills. The agent is not the only one who has product knowledge and problem-solving skills—in fact, a good agent will draw upon these resources that the customer brings to the relationship.

Naturally, this information is drawn out from the customer using speaking and listening skills. When both parties bring strong skills to the service request, the interaction can be an efficient and rewarding exchange of valuable information.

Imagine each of these skills as the legs of a table. If during any customer interaction one of these legs should falter, the table will collapse. That might sound severe, but think about it. Product knowledge and problem-solving skills are essential. Even if you have to call the customer back or refer the problem to a second-level agent, your Support Center must be able to own the service request until it is resolved. The Help Desk or Support Center must have a strong resource of high-tech skills to draw from because most of the solutions are technical in nature. If in the end you don't have the high-tech skills, the interaction will be unsuccessful. So maintaining these skills at your organization is essential.

However, the high-touch skills are also vital. As an agent, you need to communicate with customers to resolve service requests. You rely on communication to learn the definition of their problems and also to present the solutions. And even if you solve the customers' problems, if your method of communication gives them a negative feeling, they may never call you back. So high-touch skills are essential to successful customer interaction.

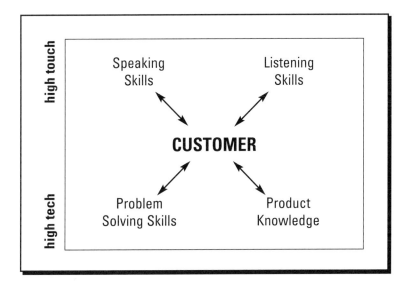

**Figure 1-1** *The customer relationship composite shows the various influences in our relationships with customers.*

To emphasize this point, consider the results of a survey that addressed why customers stop doing business, conducted by the Rockefeller Institute in Pittsburgh a few years ago. The purpose of the survey was to determine the reasons for lost accounts and to answer the question, "Why does a customer change from one supplier to another supplier?"

Figure 1-2 shows the results of the Rockefeller study. Among customers who no longer did business with a given supplier, 1% died, (if you are in sales it will always seem higher, but it's just 1%); 3% moved away; 14% formed a new business relationship (some of those are for competitive reasons, like outsourcing and other opportunities), and 14% were dissatisfied with the product. That leaves 68%—all of whom felt an attitude of indifference from one or more representatives of the supplier. So it's key that we work with our customers in a respectful way and that we learn effective

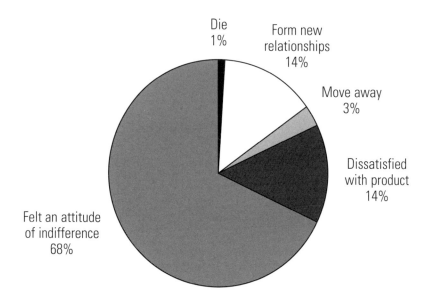

*Figure 1-2* The results of a study done by the Rockefeller Institute showing why customers move to other suppliers.

telephone communication skills. While poor communication skills can cause you to lose customers, excellent telephone communication skills can build positive and long-lasting relationships with your customers.

This book offers tips on how to improve your telephone communication skills. If you're already skilled in telephone communication, this book will help polish those skills and serve to reinforce some beneficial concepts.

# Chapter 2
## *How to create our image over the telephone*

We all grew up with telephones, and we all think we know how to use them. We've become so familiar with them, in fact, that many of us have developed bad telephone communication habits. Because of this, it's important to know and understand the differences between face-to-face communication and telephone communication. This chapter shows these surprising differences and will help you understand how we create our image over the telephone.

### The components of communication

I've coined a term I call *imageneering*. The Walt Disney Company calls some of their creative people "Imagineers," but that's not what I'm talking about here. I'm combining the words *image*, defined as "a concept or character of something or someone held by the public; a representation to the mind by speech or writing" and *engineer*, defined as, "to plan, construct, or manage by skillful acts," to form the word *imageneer*. My definition for this hybrid word is: "to construct and manage public perceptions through the spoken word; creating either a positive or negative impression."

Every time we interact with customers we are *imageneering*. Whether we care to think about it or not, we are constantly reinforcing or changing the perceptions that others have about us. In a face-to-face situation, communication happens through the avenues of body language, tone of voice, and the actual words used. But the importance of each avenue might surprise you. Figure 2-1 shows how, according to "Customer Service Skills for Help Desk Professionals" (Help Desk Institute, ©1992), visual communication – your body language, gestures, and facial

11

expressions-accounts for 55% of getting your message across. Our tone of voice, or attitude, carries 38% of our meaning. The content-the actual word choice-accounts for only 7% of our face-to-face communication.

| The avenues of verbal communication | Percentage of emphasis face-to-face |
|---|---|
| 1. Body language, gesture, facial expression | 55% |
| 2. Tone of voice | 38% |
| 3. Word content | 7% |

*Figure 2-1* How the three avenues of communication influence face-to-face communication

However, as shown in Figure 2-2, these avenues are weighted much differently when communicating over the telephone. When you're on the telephone, 55% of the communication–the visual stimulus–isn't present. Instead, 85% of telephone communication comes across in your *tone*–your attitude–or how you address the customer. And only 15% of your message gets across with your words.

| The avenues of verbal communication | Percentage of emphasis on the telephone |
|---|---|
| 1. Body language, gesture, facial expression | 0% |
| 2. Tone of voice | 85% |
| 3. Word content | 15% |

*Figure 2-2* How the three avenues of communication influence telephone communication

So, until we get some training, or really think about how powerful the telephone is, we really aren't fully serving our customers. Returning to the concept of *imageneering*, we need to understand that we create an image each time we interact with a customer over the telephone. Our goal should be to skillfully manage the perceptions we create. To do this, we need to master both listening and speaking skills.

# Chapter 3
## *Effective listening skills*

Good listening skills pay off; they present real benefits to your organization. If you're a good listener, you accomplish more in a shorter period of time because you get the right information to begin with. You reduce the margin of error because you are focused on what the customer is saying instead of what you're going to be saying next. When you listen well, the conversation stays on track and–even more valuable–*the customer likes you more*. You help build rapport with customers based on genuine interest and caring.

To learn effective listening skills, you first need to understand a few things about three components of verbal communication which are rate of speech, tone (or attitude), and the word choice It's important for you to recognize cues from all three components of verbal communication to be effective. We'll discuss these a little later in this chapter because before you can listen, you have to pay attention. You won't pick up subtle clues from a person's verbal communication if you're not paying attention. First, let's review some of the things that cause our minds to wander.

### Five factors that prevent us from listening
All of us, at one time or another, have been on the telephone with a customer and were distracted by something that caused us to miss part of the conversation. We've had to ask him or her to repeat what was said. When this has happened to you, you probably wished you had paid attention, because if you had, you would have stayed on track with the conversation. There are five reasons why we sometimes have trouble paying attention to customers. These are listed in Figure 3-1. By understanding these reasons, you'll be better able to avoid them.

### Environmental distractions

A support center can often be a "beehive" of activity. You might be on the telephone with a customer when a coworker shoves a piece of paper in your face. Or a red light may begin flashing because there are so many customers in the queue. All kinds of distractions and interruptions can take place. But in the midst of it, you need to pay attention and focus.

### The third ear syndrome

I find that many help desk and support center representatives develop a third ear. While you're on the telephone listening to the customer with two ears, you might have a "third ear" tuned in to what is going on in the background. If this happens, it might be because you care about your coworkers and customers. You might suddenly overhear another agent attempting to solve a tricky problem that you spent a lot of time solving the previous day. Or, conversely, you might hear someone solving a tricky problem you couldn't solve. While this distraction is based upon good intentions, it detracts from your ability to focus on the task at hand-resolving your current call.

1. Environmental distractions
2. The "third ear" syndrome
3. Jumping ahead
4. Emotional filters
5. Mental side trips

**Figure 3-1** *Five factors that prevent us from listening*

### Jumping ahead

Another factor that prevents us from listening is that we sometimes focus on what we are going to say next. Sometimes we mentally *jump ahead* in the conversation. This has to do with two factors. First, we are expected to solve problems as quickly as possible. Second, we can listen at a faster rate than we can speak. I'll explain more about this concept later.

### Emotional filters

Some support organizations serve the same customer base all the time. Because of this, you may get to know some of your customers and develop an emotional response to them. These are called *emotional filters*. For example, you might have a perception that a particular customer is always angry. Because of this, you might "brace yourself" whenever that customer calls. I'm sure you understand how this can unfairly influence the transaction. Good listeners are careful to avoid this. You need to keep an open mind from the beginning of every conversation.

### Mental side trips

Another reason we don't pay attention is because of *mental side trips*. Here's an example of a mental side trip. Let's say it's about 11:30 in the morning, and you get the type of call you've been handling all day long. You know what the customer is going to say; you've handled a number of these calls already. Now you're wondering, "where am I going for lunch?" You re-engage yourself in the conversation and find that you haven't lost too much. The customer continues to talk, and you work together to define the problem. Maybe you think you know what the customer is going to say next, so you decide you're going to eat lunch at a certain restaurant because it's next door to a shop you'd like to visit. You start thinking about what you are going to buy, and so on. Now you're on a mental side trip. You come back into the conversation, and you've lost it. Your mental side trip has gone on for too long. You've wasted time, and you have to backtrack in the conversation by asking the customer to repeat what was said. This often happens because we think much more quickly than we talk. Just being aware of this tendency will help you hang in with what the customer is saying.

## The three components of verbal communication

The three components of verbal communication are rate of speech, tone, and word choice. Don't confuse these with the three *avenues* of communication that I discussed earlier. The *avenues* are actually three different modes of communication. Even though some of the *components* are the same, I'm referring to them as ways verbal communication can be measured, analyzed, and adjusted.

### Rate of speech
A newscaster speaks an average of 125 to 150 words per minute. The rate of speech among most English-speaking people will vary, but generally will be about 125 to 150 words per minute. This fact doesn't mean much until you consider that we comprehend what we hear at a rate of 300 words per minute. So we can actually absorb information much faster than we can speak. But we can think even faster—an estimated rate of 500 words a minute! If you're not careful, you'll find yourself racing ahead or finishing your customers' sentences for them. If someone isn't talking fast enough, you might subconsciously say "Just let *me* tell *you* what *you* were going to tell *me*, and we'll get it done faster."

A good listener will not only recognize the rate of someone's speech, but be able to understand more about the customer's emotional needs based on that rate of speech as well. A slower rate of speech might indicate confusion or fatigue. A faster rate of speech might indicate anger or impatience. Then again, these indications might be misleading. But listening closely to your customer's rate of speech will make you a more effective communicator.

To measure your own rate of speech and make sure you're not speaking too quickly or too slowly, I've included a quick exercise in Figure 3-2.

### Tone
Remember, 85% of verbal communication happens through our tone (or our attitude). This concept was stated well in a commercial I recently saw. In that commercial, a sales representative said, "They don't care what you know, until they know you care." This is especially true of your customers in a service situation. Customers want solutions to their technical problems, but they often have emotional needs as well. We need to address both types of needs. They may not be effective or productive that day until we can get them back on line, both technically and emotionally.

A good listener will hear the emotional needs communicated through customer's tone. A sigh might mean the customer is frustrated or tired. Laughter might mean the customer is embarrassed or intimidated. Listening closely will give you insight into the best ways to respond to their emotional needs.

**Am I speaking too fast?**
For that matter, am I speaking too slowly? The following paragraph is 156 words long. By reading it aloud at your normal rate of speech, you will be able to gauge your rate of speech against the average of 125-150. Test yourself briefly...the results may surprise you!

**One Minute Statement**
Most experts agree that the ideal rate of speech is between one hundred and twenty-five and one hundred and fifty words per minute. At this rate, people who are listening to you will be able to understand you easily. Over the telephone your voice carries eighty-five percent of the message you wish to convey. Therefore it is important to speak at an acceptable rate. Since the remaining fifteen percent of the message is conveyed by the actual content, choose your words wisely. With every telephone call, you create an image of you and your organization. Be sure the image you create is favorable so that your customers will want to call again. You know what other people sound like on the telephone. How do you sound? Sincere or insincere? Interested or indifferent? Take the time to evaluate how you come across. If you read this statement in one minute, your speech rate is excellent.

*Figure 3-2* An exercise to measure rate of speech

*Word content*
The third component of verbal communication is the words the speaker chooses. As a listener, you can understand much about a technical problem as well as a customer's emotional state based

on the words he or she chooses. Improper use of technical words might indicate the customer has a lower level of expertise. Excessive "you" or "me" language might give you insight into the behavioral style the customer is using, which we'll discuss more about in Chapter 4.

## Seven listening "do's"

There are seven listening "do's" that will help you become a more effective listener. These are listed in Figure 3-3.

### Pay attention

We've covered this already, but it needs to be emphasized. Nothing is more important than paying attention.

| | |
|---|---|
| 1. Pay attention | 5. Assess the customer's |
| 2. Listen for ideas | level of expertise |
| 3. Take notes | 6. Read between the lines |
| 4. Assess the customer's | 7. Listen for "unspoken" |
| emotional state | service requests |

**Figure 3-3** *The seven "listening do's" that lead to more effective telephone communication*

### Listen for ideas

Sometimes a customer verbally communicates in a manner that is distracting or amusing. Any number of speech idiosyncrasies can become a distraction–speaking excessively fast or slow, having an extremely high or low pitch, using an excessive vocabulary, or speaking with a heavy accent. You need to resist the temptation to be entertained or distracted by the speaker and listen for ideas and central themes.

### Take notes

You probably already know to do this, but it's easy to get out of the habit. Taking notes will help keep you more focused. Jot down major points or the parameters of a problem to help keep you involved. Some people even draw pictures, such as flow charting, diagramming, or storyboarding. By combining words and images, you can sometimes improve both your listening and problem-solving skills. Find your own ways to stay attentive to a particular call.

### Assess the customer's emotional state

We've already covered this indirectly, but it's an important issue. We have no idea of the history of a given service request when the telephone rings. The customer on the other end might have worked a long time to solve a problem and might be quite frustrated by the time he or she calls you. The only way you can determine the customer's emotional state is by listening. Listen to tone of voice, listen to rate of speech, and listen to the words chosen. A good listener can pinpoint whether a customer is frustrated, bored, angry, or afraid.

### Assess the customer's level of expertise

Again, you do this by listening. A good way to tell customers' level of expertise is by listening to their vocabulary, their understanding of the problem, and the type of information they offer. When solving customers' problems, it's very valuable to know if they are novices or a power-users. If a customer is a power user, the solution might be as simple as telling him or her, "You need to change the number of files in your config.sys to 200." Imagine spending several minutes on the telephone telling a highly-skilled programmer how to create a backup of the config.sys file! Knowing your customer's level of expertise can save a lot of time.

### Read between the lines

Sometimes you need to listen to what *isn't* being said. For example, if a customer calls in and says, "I have this problem reformatting my disk. I just looked in the manual, and they told me to do such and such. Now, what else do I need to do?" If you've listened carefully, alarms should be going off in your mind. You should always sit up and take notice when someone says they are reformatting a disk. You know what disasters could happen if he or she makes a mistake. So its your responsibility to ask them, "What do you want to accomplish? Why are you doing this?" The customer has asked a question that would necessarily make us ask that, but we need to read between the lines. After all, if a customer does destroy data, who will often get the blame? The support center agent that offered the advice.

### Listen for other "unspoken" service requests
These are sometimes extremely subtle, but once customers get you on the telephone, they often unload a litany of problems onto you. Some of these problems won't "belong" to you, but write them down as they come up anyway. For example, Tom Smith might call you because he is having a memory problem with Windows. While you're stepping him through a procedure to help manage his computer's memory, Tom might say, "You know, the last time I did that, my computer locked up and I lost my help file." Or, he might say, "By the way, I heard so-and-so got the latest version of Microsoft Word. I heard it can do some great stuff." These are *unspoken* service requests. Tom is telling you about them for a reason. Imagine how he will react if, at the end of the conversation, you say, "By the way, I'll send a new copy of the help.txt file through e-mail, and I'll notify inventory management that you're interested in getting the latest version of Word." So by listening for these subtle service requests, you can go a long way toward creating a loyal customer.

## Three listening "don'ts"
I learned most of these lessons the hard way. If I'm not careful, I will interrupt customers. I will often finish their sentences for them. I am also prone to talking too quickly. I've made all of the following mistakes, and everybody, even the best customer service agent, does. Nevertheless, by being aware of these mistakes, listed in Figure 3-4, you will hopefully commit these "listening don'ts" less often.

### Don't interrupt
This is particularly important with an irate caller. You really want to let irate callers tell you their story—as painful as that

might be sometimes. By letting them tell their story you help them get their frustration off their chest. If you interrupt them or try to "cut to the chase," you might solve their problem, but they might still feel discouraged.

---

1. Don't interrupt
2. Don't finish a customer's sentence
3. Don't assume

---

*Figure 3-4*  *Three "listening don'ts" to avoid during telephone communication*

### Don't finish a customer's sentence

We already know that if we're prone to finish a customer's sentence, it's probably because we're thinking ahead. Since we know what we are doing and have experience with many customers' problems, some problems become quite routine. Remember to resist the temptation to tell customers the moment you know the solution to their problem. They may find this belittling. And if you're incorrect, you'll embarrass yourself and detract from your credibility. So hang in there and listen to the content.

### Don't assume

This "listening don't" is similar to the previous point. Sometimes a customer will give you the general parameters of a problem. Sue Jones might say, "my report is printing out...but it's so light I can barely read it." You might assume and tell her, "Change the toner cartridge. Bye!" However, you need to avoid solving a problem until you know all the facts. A minute later, Sue might call back saying, "I replaced the toner cartridge, and it's still printing light." Now you've wasted time, wasted an expensive toner cartridge, and frustrated the customer. By asking a few more questions, you might have found out that Sue's text was formatted to print gray instead of black or some other factor was affecting the print quality. Never assume.

## Conclusion

When thinking about "communication skills," many people immediately think about speaking. They think about formulating sentences well, using eloquent words, or being succinct or funny. But the best path toward being a good communicator is to be "quick to listen and slow to speak." Listening skills are more important than most people realize. Those who do realize it are probably the best communicators.

# Chapter 4
*Effective speaking skills*

While listening skills are vital, they are only half the effort. Eventually, we are going to have to respond. The good news is that much of what we learned in the Chapter 3 can also be applied to good speaking skills.

The reason why speaking skills are so important can be summed up nicely in one of my favorite quotes, which is attributed to Will Rogers. He said, "Speak with words that are soft and sweet, you never know when you have to eat them." If you've ever been harsh or rude with a customer, you probably know this lesson well. Rude words can end up haunting us. So always address customers respectfully and professionally.

This chapter is devoted to giving you practical ways to *imageneer* the best possible image for yourself and your organization through the way you speak. First, we will quickly review the three communication behavioral styles, then we will discuss some valuable do's and don'ts for telephone communication.

## Three communication behavioral styles

We are going to briefly look at three basic communication styles, which are listed in Figure 4-1. Our behavioral style can dictate, in large part, the attitude that comes across in our communication.

One good definition of the word *attitude* is: "A state of mind or feeling with regard to some matter or somebody. Or, our disposition." Remember, our attitude, or tone, makes up 85% of the message we convey to our customers over the telephone. Our attitude speaks the loudest.

*Passive*
The first behavioral style I'm going to discuss is *passive*. Passive people are characterized by over-agreeing. If someone is "yessing" you, he or she probably has a more passive communication style. Passive people are also characterized by sacrificing behavior. You may know someone who always takes on too much work. They are always saying, "yes, I can do that, and that, and that. I will do that, and that, too." By the end of the week, they can't possibly get through all the projects and all the call-backs they've committed to. You should avoid being passive with customers or with management. In short, passive people *underuse* their personal power. They don't stand up for their rights.

Sometimes the pressure builds up in passive people and they blow up–suddenly exhibiting aggressive behavior.

*Aggressive*
This behavioral style is characterized by dominating language. Aggressive people blame others. They use phrases like "*you* should, *you* are wrong, it's *your* fault." They choose language that can humiliate and threaten others. Aggressive communication tends to be adversarial, excluding the other person from the problem-solving process.

1. Passive
2. Aggressive
3. Assertive

*Figure 4-1*  *Three communication behavioral styles*

Aggressive people overuse their personal power. They have no trouble standing up for their own rights, but they may often trample on the rights of others.

## Assertive

The most desirable behavioral style is the *assertive* mode. This behavioral style is characterized by *I* statements and *we* statements. Assertive people use direct, positive, participatory language. Instead of being blame-oriented, assertive people are results-oriented. Disagreements are seen as a constructive means of learning. Assertive people stand up for their own rights, but understand and respect the rights of others. In fact, assertive language is really the accepted language in business today. Whether you are talking with customers, delegating, working with peers, or working with supervisors and management, you should communicate assertively.

## The benefits of assertiveness

Assertive people are pleasant to talk to. They don't get defensive or accusatory. They always look for the good in people because they are capable of seeing the good in *themselves*. Assertive people respect and care about their customers. After talking with an assertive person, customers often feel valued and confident that their service requests will be addressed. Plus, when you're assertive, you'll often arrive at a better solution because both you and your customer have participated.

It's *healthy* to be assertive, too. In the 1950's a psychiatrist named Dr. Joseph Wolpe did a study on assertive behavior and assertive communication. He wanted to see if his patients, who were dealing with anxiety, exhibited any physiological effects by using assertive behavior and assertive communication. Using biofeedback techniques, he found that anxiety is reduced when people use assertive communication by standing up for themselves. In fact, assertiveness and anxiety are incompatible behaviors.

Help Desks and Support Centers can be very stressful environments. I don't need to get into the reasons why; you know the reasons. The point is, you can become anxious or stressed on the job. When you are in an assertive mode, however, your stress levels decrease. So, the customer not only benefits from your assertive behavior, but your health benefits as well.

Another benefit of assertive behavior is that it adds credibility. You can only resolve a problem when your customer accepts the solution you offer. The customers will be more likely to accept your solution if he or she feels you are a credible source. Assertive communication creates credibility because assertive people sound more confident. Also, if you make your customers feel respected, they won't be as resistant to your advice.

If you're assertive, your customers will be far less likely to end up in that 68% of customers who felt there was an attitude of indifference on the part of the representative. And you'll be more likely to build positive, ongoing relationships. Since customers talk to each other, they might be telling other people about the positive experience they've had with your help desk or support center. That improves your image even more.

## Seven "speaking do's"
Figure 4-2 lists seven speaking "do's" to remember when communicating over the telephone.

### Smile
You may be tired of hearing it, but it's a good idea to smile. When you're on the telephone, imagine yourself talking face-to-face with the person. If you literally smile and show enthusiasm, you'll convey a more pleasant attitude by the tone of your voice. You may think I'm contradicting myself, since I explained earlier that body language does not play a part in telephone communication, but this is an exception. Even though your customer doesn't see

| | |
|---|---|
| 1. Smile | 5. Acknowledge the customer and the problem |
| 2. Use the callers name | |
| 3. Echo important points | 6. Mirror your customers |
| 4. Incorporate courteous remarks | 7. Tape or monitor calls |

*Figure 4-2* Seven "speaking do's" that contribute to more effective telephone communication

you, your posture, body language, and facial expression will be communicated through the tone of your voice. The fact is, our hearing is so attuned to subtleties of speech that people can tell if you are smiling. Likewise, your customer can tell if you feel exhausted and are slouching at your desk. Customers can hear our attitude in our tone. The good news is that "feelings follow actions." If you force yourself to smile, you will actually begin feeling more enthusiastic. It sounds absurd, but it's true. In fact, some agents put a mirror at their workstation as a reminder to smile. Do whatever you can to monitor your attitude, and the interactions with your customers will improve.

### Use the caller's name

This helps you establish rapport. Using names can really have a powerful effect. When I'm calling for support and the agent uses my name in the conversation, it makes me feel more valued–like I'm an individual and the agent cares enough about *me* to remember my name. Suddenly I feel more engaged in the conversation. Of course, whether you use first or last names depends on the type of service you offer and the culture of your organization. Using first names has a more powerful effect, but using last names can also be effective. One rule of thumb is to address the customer the way they introduce themselves to you. If the customer said, "Hi, this Dr. Robert Walker in the lab," then address him thereafter as "Doctor Walker." Don't call him "Bob."

### Echo important points

After your customer describes a problem, it is often valuable to "echo" what they said–especially if you're not completely sure of what they said. Repeat the main points to them. Use statements like "So, you're saying that after you saved the file, you reopened it and your changes weren't reflected?" You might often find that you haven't understood correctly or that the customer didn't phrase the situation exactly right. This practice will not only keep you engaged in the conversation but will reassure the customer and possibly save time by preventing you from going down blind alleys.

### Incorporate courteous remarks

This may sound like the Emily Post School of Customer Service, but politeness works. Words like "thank you," "please," "I'm glad to help you," are simple and make a big difference. You will consistently leave customers with a better feeling and with the perception that your organization is staffed by courteous, helpful people.

### Acknowledge the customer and the problem

Directly address the emotional need of the customer and their need for a solution. Try to use empathetic, assertive statements such as, "That happened to me once. It was really frustrating. Now let's see if we can't solve this..." This comes back to the saying "they don't care what you know, until they know you care." Often, a customers call feeling frustrated with technology or that they've has been treated unjustly, or that they've reached the end of their rope. By acknowledging their emotional state and empathizing with it, you can meet their emotional needs. Then, you can steer the conversation toward solving the problem at hand.

### Mirror your customer

Here's where your listening skills can be used most effectively. Listen to your customers and *mirror* their vocabulary, their rate of speech, and their point of view. If your customer is a novice and uses simple language, you want to match that, and keep things on a basic level. If a customer is talking slowly, gear down and talk slowly so he or she can grasp the information needed. And, when it is appropriate, try to mirror your customer's point of view. Remember, your job isn't to win arguments, it's to solve the customer's problem. So put yourself in your customer's shoes. Naturally, you don't have to agree, if they feel that all "computer people" are evil. But you don't have to verbalize your disagreement either. Instead, find common ground and start there. Use empathetic statements like "Yes, we computer folks can sometimes be out of touch." By doing this, you're steering your customer into an agreeable mode. Once you mirror your customer in this way, you can maneuver the conversation into a problem-solving context.

*Tape or monitor your calls*
Some customer service organizations use silent monitoring systems to monitor their calls. This is an excellent way to provide feedback to agents. By taping your calls, you can hear how you are coming across. If you've ever recorded your calls, you've probably been very surprised to hear what you really sound like. Whether it's the pitch or volume of your voice, or your word choices, you might suddenly hear nuances in your voice that imply an attitude you don't intend. In short, you might be surprised by how you sound.

You can tape your calls without getting permission or consent from the customer by bringing in a cassette recorder and setting it next to you while you answer calls. You can't hear what the customer is saying, but just knowing how you sound can greatly improve your telephone communication skills. If your organization has monitoring in place, ask to hear your calls so you can self-correct. If you want, you can listen to the tapes with a peer or a supervisor to get feedback from them. But you'll be surprised how little coaching you'll need to improve your speaking skills. You'll probably be able to hear for yourself what speaking and listening skills you need to improve.

## Four speaking "don'ts"
There are four speaking "don'ts" to remember when interacting with customers. These are listed in Figure 4-3.

```
1. Don't use jargon or abbreviations
2. Don't mumble
3. Don't use negative language
4. Don't argue
```

*Figure 4-3* Four "speaking don'ts" to avoid

### Don't use jargon or acronyms

In my work with customer support centers, I've found that every organization has different acronyms. When you live with certain acronyms every day, it's easy to incorporate them into your everyday vocabulary. We often make the mistake of assuming that words that are common to us are common to everybody. So don't say, "Bob over in SWD wants to upgrade the BRQ; until then, switch over to the YBTM, okay?" This kind of alphabet soup is likely to baffle your customer. And, even worse, customers will sometimes pretend to know what you're talking about so don't look stupid. If you think about it, you'll realize that the end-result of this can impede communication on many levels. Think about your vocabulary. Speak as clearly as possible, even if you have to say the whole word or define a word.

### Don't mumble

Be careful not to mumble. It's difficult to enunciate if you're chewing while you're talking. This will aggravate your customers, make them feel less important, and decrease the efficiency of your communication. Unclear communication also detracts from your professional image, and the image of your support organization.

### Don't use negative language

Phrases like "we can't do that" or "we won't do that" can damage the reputation of your support organization and frustrate your customers. Always focus on what you *can* do—what your action plan will be in working with the customer.

Another phrase to avoid is "that's our policy." Customers dislike the word "policy." Nobody wants to hear "policy" as an excuse for not getting something done. Service level agreements are another matter, and sometimes you'll need to reinforce a portion of this agreement.

"You're wrong" is definitely a phrase to avoid. Not only should you avoid saying this outright, but don't communicate it in the tone of your voice. Sometimes the way you phrase a statement or instruction can be interpreted by your customer as "no, no, no, you're wrong." Be careful to avoid this implication.

Also, avoid using the phrase, "I'll try." Customers don't want you to *try*, they want you to *do*. They want action and results. So even if you know the best you can do is try, find a way to phrase that positively. Say, "Here's what we'll do, and I'll get back to you." It sounds more positive and won't cause the customer to react.

Another speaking don't is, "I'll have to ask my supervisor." Don't give away your power if you don't have to. You could simply say, "I'll research this and call you back." Then set a time frame. If you're going to pass the situation on to second-level support, let your customer know you're going to do it.

These five phrases are listed again in Figure 4-4. Be careful to avoid them.

1. "I won't /can't do that."
2. "That's our policy."
3. "You're wrong."
4. "I'll try."
5. "I'll have to ask my supervisor."

*Figure 4-4* *Five phrases to avoid with customers*

### Don't argue

Never ever argue with a customer. The L.L. Bean Company developed a poster that shows why this is important. It was called "What is a Customer?" At one time, this poster was up in everyone's workspace. A few of the points from this poster illustrate why it's wrong to argue with a customer.

A customer is the most important person ever in this office...
The customer is not dependent on us, we are dependent on him...
Nobody has ever won an argument with a customer.

Whatever "ego boost" you might gain by winning an argument with a customer is far outweighed by the harm it can do your business. After all, as the L.L. Bean poster also reads:

> A customer is a person who brings us his wants. It's our job to handle them profitably for him and for ourselves.

## Conclusion

Good telephone communication skills are worth learning. They help create more satisfied customers, and this can increase the perceived and actual value of your support organization. Effective telephone communication skills also help you solve problems more quickly and efficiently. By employing the techniques of good speaking and good listening, and by adapting assertive behavior when dealing with customers, you will help your help desk or support center make a substantial impact on the bottom line of your larger organization.

NOTES